QWEN 2.5

THE NEXT-GEN AI - A DEEP DIVE INTO LARGE LANGUAGE MODELS

OLIVER LUCAS JR

TABLE OF CONTENTS

Chapter 1

Chapter 2

Chapter 3

Chapter 4

Chapter 5

Chapter 6

Chapter 7

Chapter 8

Chapter 9

Chapter 10

locking the Power of Language: A Guide to Qwen 2.5

Welcome to the exciting world of large language models! This book serves as your comprehensive guide to Qwen 2.5, a cutting-edge language model developed by Alibaba Cloud. Whether you're a seasoned AI researcher, a curious developer, or simply fascinated by the potential of artificial intelligence, this book will equip you with the knowledge and skills to harness the power of Qwen 2.5.

Within these pages, we'll embark on a journey that explores the intricacies of Qwen 2.5, from its underlying architecture and capabilities to its diverse applications and ethical considerations. We'll delve into the art of prompt engineering, guiding you to craft effective prompts that unlock the model's full potential. We'll examine real-world use cases, showcasing how Qwen 2.5 can be applied to content creation, code generation, data analysis, and more.

This book is not just a theoretical exploration; it's a practical handbook designed to empower you to experiment, build, and innovate with Qwen 2.5. We'll provide you with the tools and resources you need to get started, including code examples, tutorials, and links to online communities.

As you delve into the world of Qwen 2.5, we encourage you to approach this technology with a sense of curiosity, responsibility, and a commitment to ethical AI development. By understanding the capabilities and limitations of LLMs, we can harness their power to create a more informed, creative, and equitable future.

We hope this book serves as your trusted companion on your Qwen 2.5 journey. Let's begin!

Chapter 1

Introduction to Qwen 2.5

1.1 The Evolution of Large Language Models

The Early Days of Language Modeling

Imagine teaching a computer to speak. Sounds like science fiction, right? But that's exactly what researchers started trying to do decades ago. This section explores those early attempts, the challenges they faced, and how they paved the way for the powerful language models we have today.

Rule-Based Systems: The "Grammar Police" of Language

Think of these early systems as the strict grammar teachers of the AI world. They relied on meticulously handcrafted rules and dictionaries. Essentially, researchers tried to program every grammatical rule and exception into the computer, hoping it would then understand and generate human-like text.

Example: A rule might be, "Add an 's' to a noun to make it plural." But language is messy! What about irregular plurals like "children" or "mice"? These systems often stumbled over such complexities.

Statistical Language Models (SLMs): Letting the Data Speak

Instead of relying solely on rules, SLMs took a different approach. They analyzed massive amounts of text data to identify patterns and probabilities.

Think of it like this: If you read thousands of books, you'd start to get a feel for which words often appear together. SLMs did something similar, using a technique called "n-grams" to analyze sequences of words. For example, a 3-gram model would look at sequences of three words to predict the next word in a sentence.

Challenges and Limitations: Hitting a Wall

Despite these early efforts, significant hurdles remained.

Data Sparsity: These models were data-hungry, requiring enormous amounts of text to learn effectively. But in those early days, such vast datasets weren't always readily available.

Lack of Context: Early models struggled to understand the meaning and context of words. They might generate grammatically correct sentences that made little sense.

The Takeaway

These early language models, while limited, were crucial stepping stones. They laid the groundwork for the more sophisticated approaches that would follow, paving the way for the neural network revolution and the rise of large language models like Qwen 2.5.

Key improvements for clarity and engagement:

Analogies and metaphors: Using comparisons like the "grammar police" and reading thousands of books helps make complex ideas more relatable.

Simple language: Avoiding overly technical jargon makes the content accessible to a wider audience.

Clear explanations: Breaking down concepts into smaller, digestible chunks aids understanding.

Emphasis on the "why": Explaining the motivations behind each approach helps readers grasp the overall narrative of language model evolution.

I'm ready to continue collaborating on the next sections! Let me know what you'd like to tackle next.

1.2 What Makes Qwen 2.5 Unique?

Qwen 2.5 isn't just another large language model. It builds upon the successes of its predecessors and incorporates cutting-edge advancements to stand out in the crowded field of LLMs. Here's what makes it truly unique:

Enhanced Reasoning and Problem-Solving: Qwen 2.5 demonstrates significant improvements in logical reasoning and problem-solving tasks. It can tackle complex questions, analyze information, and generate creative solutions more effectively than previous versions. This is due to architectural refinements and a focus on training with datasets that emphasize logical thinking.

Expanded Context Window: One of the most striking features of Qwen 2.5 is its massive context window. It can "remember" and process much longer chunks of text, allowing for more coherent and informed responses in conversations and text generation tasks. This expanded context window also enables Qwen 2.5 to handle complex, multi-step instructions and maintain a consistent understanding of the conversation flow.

Multi-Modality: Bridging the Gap Between Text and Code: Qwen 2.5 excels at understanding and generating both natural language and programming code. It can translate between languages, explain code snippets, and even generate code in various programming languages. This multi-modal capability opens up exciting possibilities for developers and researchers, allowing them to leverage Qwen 2.5 for tasks like code auto-completion, bug detection, and code generation.

Focus on Openness and Accessibility: While many powerful LLMs are proprietary, Qwen 2.5 emphasizes open access. This commitment to openness fosters collaboration and allows developers and researchers to experiment with and build upon the model's capabilities. This accessibility can drive innovation and accelerate the development of new AI applications.

Continuous Improvement and Refinement: The development of Qwen 2.5 is an ongoing journey. The team behind it is constantly working on improvements, incorporating the latest research findings and user feedback. This commitment to continuous learning ensures that Qwen 2.5 remains at the forefront of LLM technology.

In essence, Qwen 2.5 distinguishes itself through:

Superior reasoning abilities

Vast context window

Multi-modal capabilities

Open access

Continuous improvement

These qualities make Qwen 2.5 a powerful and versatile tool for a wide range of applications, from chatbots and content creation to code generation and scientific research.

1.3 Applications and Potential of Qwen 2.5

Qwen 2.5 isn't just a theoretical marvel; it's a powerful tool with the potential to revolutionize various fields. Its unique capabilities open doors to a wide range of applications across industries:

1.3.1 Transforming Communication and Content Creation:

Elevated Chatbots and Virtual Assistants: Qwen 2.5 can power more intelligent and engaging chatbots, capable of understanding complex requests, providing personalized responses, and even offering emotional support. Imagine virtual assistants that can truly understand your needs and preferences.

Creative Writing and Content Generation: From writing stories and poems to generating marketing copy and scripts, Qwen 2.5 can assist writers and content creators in producing high-quality, engaging content. It can even help overcome writer's block by offering suggestions and generating different creative text formats.

Seamless Language Translation: Qwen 2.5's multilingual capabilities can break down language barriers, enabling real-time translation for communication and facilitating global collaboration. Imagine a world where language is no longer a barrier to understanding.

1.3.2 Boosting Productivity and Efficiency:

Streamlined Code Development: Qwen 2.5 can assist developers in writing, debugging, and optimizing code, increasing productivity and reducing development time. Imagine a coding assistant that can anticipate your needs and suggest code snippets.

Automated Content Summarization: Qwen 2.5 can quickly summarize lengthy documents, extracting key information and saving valuable time for researchers, students, and professionals. Imagine getting the gist of a 100-page report in just a few minutes.

Personalized Learning and Education: Qwen 2.5 can create interactive learning experiences, provide personalized feedback, and adapt to individual learning styles. Imagine a tutor that can tailor lessons to your specific needs and pace.

1.3.3 Driving Innovation and Scientific Discovery:

Accelerated Research and Development: Qwen 2.5 can analyze vast amounts of scientific literature, identify research gaps, and even generate hypotheses, accelerating the pace of scientific discovery. Imagine a research assistant that can sift through thousands of papers to find the most relevant information.

Drug Discovery and Development: Qwen 2.5 can analyze biological data, predict drug interactions, and assist in the development of new treatments and therapies. Imagine using AI to accelerate the search for cures for diseases.

Advanced Data Analysis and Insights: Qwen 2.5 can analyze complex datasets, identify trends, and generate insights, helping businesses make informed decisions. Imagine an AI that can predict market trends and optimize business strategies.

1.3.4 The Future Potential of Qwen 2.5:

The potential of Qwen 2.5 extends far beyond these examples. As the model continues to evolve, we can expect even more innovative applications in fields like:

Personalized Healthcare: Imagine AI-powered systems that can provide personalized medical advice and monitor your health.

Smart Cities and Infrastructure: Imagine cities that use AI to optimize traffic flow, manage resources, and improve public safety.

Human-Computer Interaction: Imagine interacting with computers using natural language, making technology more accessible and intuitive.

Qwen 2.5 is poised to play a key role in shaping the future of AI and its impact on our lives. By understanding its potential, we can harness its power to create a more innovative, efficient, and equitable world.

Chapter 2

The Architecture of Qwen 2.5

2.1 Transformers and Attention Mechanisms

Imagine you're reading a sentence. You don't focus on each word in isolation, right? You pay attention to how words relate to each other, which words are most important, and how they contribute to the overall meaning. That's the basic idea behind attention mechanisms in AI.

The Problem with Traditional Models

Before Transformers, models like Recurrent Neural Networks (RNNs) were commonly used for language processing. But RNNs had a limitation: they processed words one by one, in a sequence. This made it difficult for them to capture long-range dependencies between words that were far apart in a sentence.

Enter the Transformer

The Transformer architecture, introduced in 2017, revolutionized language modeling by replacing sequential processing with a mechanism called "self-attention."

Self-Attention: The Key to Understanding Relationships

Self-attention allows the model to consider all words in a sentence simultaneously when processing each word. It's like the model can "look at" all the words at once and figure out how they relate to each other.

This enables the model to capture long-range dependencies and understand the context of each word more effectively.

How Attention Works

1 Calculating Importance: For each word, the model calculates "attention scores" that represent how much it should "pay attention" to other words in the sentence.

2 Weighted Sum: These attention scores are used to create a weighted sum of the representations of all the words. This weighted sum captures the context of the word being processed.

Multi-Head Attention: Seeing from Different Perspectives

Transformers often use "multi-head attention," which is like having multiple sets of eyes looking at the sentence from different angles. Each "head" focuses on different aspects of the relationships between words, allowing the model to capture a richer understanding of the text.

Why Transformers are a Game-Changer

Parallel Processing: Transformers can process all words in a sentence at the same time, making them much faster than RNNs.

Long-Range Dependencies: They excel at capturing relationships between words that are far apart, leading to better understanding of context and meaning.

Improved Performance: Transformers have achieved state-of-the-art results on a wide range of language tasks, including translation, summarization, and question answering.

In the context of Qwen 2.5:

The Transformer architecture is the foundation of Qwen 2.5's powerful language processing capabilities. Its attention mechanisms enable it to understand complex relationships between words, capture long-range dependencies, and generate human-like text with remarkable accuracy.

This section provides a foundational understanding of Transformers and attention mechanisms, setting the stage for a deeper dive into Qwen 2.5's architecture and capabilities in the following sections.

2.2 Decoding the Inner Workings of Qwen 2.5

While we can't delve into every intricate detail of Qwen 2.5's architecture (some of that is proprietary magic!), we can explore the key components and mechanisms that make it tick.

Building Blocks: The Transformer Foundation

At its core, Qwen 2.5, like many modern LLMs, is built upon the Transformer architecture. This means it relies heavily on the attention mechanism we discussed earlier. But Qwen 2.5 takes it further with some unique tweaks and enhancements.

Key Architectural Components:

1 Embedding Layer: This is where words are converted into numerical representations (vectors) that the model can understand. Qwen 2.5 likely uses advanced embedding techniques to capture semantic relationships between words.

2 Encoder-Decoder Structure:

Encoder: This part of the model processes the input text, breaking it down and understanding its meaning using multiple layers of self-attention and feed-forward neural networks. Qwen 2.5's encoder is likely deeper and more complex than its predecessors, allowing it to capture more nuanced information.

Decoder: This part generates the output text, word by word, based on the information extracted by the encoder. It also uses self-attention to focus on relevant parts of the input and previously generated text.

3 Positional Encodings: Since Transformers process words in parallel, they need a way to understand the order of words in a sentence. Positional encodings provide this information, allowing the model to capture the sequential nature of language.

4 Layer Normalization and Residual Connections: These techniques help stabilize training and improve the flow of information through the model, contributing to its overall performance.

Qwen 2.5's Unique Enhancements:

Improved Attention Mechanisms: Qwen 2.5 likely incorporates refinements to the attention mechanism, allowing it to capture even more complex relationships between words and handle longer sequences of text.

Enhanced Memory Mechanisms: The expanded context window suggests that Qwen 2.5 has improved memory mechanisms that allow it to "remember" and utilize information from much earlier in a conversation or document.

Multi-Modal Processing: Qwen 2.5's ability to handle both text and code suggests specialized modules within its architecture for processing different modalities.

The Training Process: A Data Feast

Qwen 2.5 is trained on a massive dataset of text and code, likely encompassing a diverse range of sources, from books and articles to code repositories and websites. This vast dataset allows the model to learn patterns, relationships, and rules of language and code.

Fine-Tuning for Specific Tasks:

After pre-training on the massive dataset, Qwen 2.5 can be fine-tuned for specific tasks, such as translation, summarization, or question answering. This involves training the model on a smaller, task-specific dataset to optimize its performance for that particular application.

The Black Box Element

While we can understand the general architecture and training process, some aspects of Qwen 2.5 remain a "black box." The exact details of its internal workings, including the specific algorithms and parameters used, are likely proprietary knowledge.

The Takeaway

Qwen 2.5 is a complex and sophisticated model with a unique architecture and training process. By understanding its key components and mechanisms, we can gain a deeper appreciation for its capabilities and potential.

2.3 A Comparison with Other LLMs

Qwen 2.5 exists in a vibrant ecosystem of large language models, each with its strengths and weaknesses. To truly understand its place in the AI landscape, let's compare it to some of its notable counterparts.

Key Players in the LLM Arena:

GPT-4 (OpenAI): A highly advanced LLM known for its impressive language generation, reasoning, and multi-modal capabilities. It excels in tasks like creative writing, code generation, and answering complex questions.

Bard (Google AI): Google's flagship LLM, known for its strong information retrieval and summarization capabilities. It leverages Google Search to access and process real-time information.

LLaMA 2 (Meta): An open-source LLM family focused on research and commercial applications. It offers various model sizes with different performance characteristics.

Claude (Anthropic): An LLM designed with a focus on safety and helpfulness. It aims to generate responses that are harmless, helpful, and honest.

Comparing Qwen 2.5:

Feature	Qwen 2.5	GPT-4	Bard	LLaMA 2	Claude
Context Window	1 million tokens	8,192 tokens (32,768 tokens in extended version)	Unknown, but likely large	Up to 4,096 tokens	100,000 tokens
Reasoning & Problem-Solving	Strong, with focus on logical thinking	Very strong	Strong, with access to Google	Good	Strong, with focus on safety

			Search		
Multi-Modality	Text and code	Text and images	Text, with some image capabilities	Primarily text	Primarily text
Openness	Open access for research and development	Limited access through API	Limited access	Open-source	Limited access through API
Strengths	Large context window, multi-modal capabilities, open access	Exceptional language generation, strong reasoning	Information retrieval, summarization	Versatility, open-source	Safety, helpfulness

Weaknesses	May still have limitations in certain complex reasoning tasks	Limited context window, restricted access	Potential biases from web data	May require fine-tuning for optimal performance	May be overly cautious in some situations

Key Takeaways:

Context Window: Qwen 2.5 boasts a significantly larger context window than most other LLMs, allowing it to handle longer conversations and documents.

Openness: Qwen 2.5's commitment to open access fosters collaboration and innovation in the LLM space.

Multi-Modality: Qwen 2.5's strength in both text and code makes it a versatile tool for various applications.

Performance: While Qwen 2.5 demonstrates strong reasoning and language generation capabilities, it's essential to consider its strengths and weaknesses in comparison to other LLMs when choosing the right model for a specific task.

This comparison provides a high-level overview of Qwen 2.5's position in the LLM landscape. It's important to note that the field is rapidly evolving, with new models and advancements emerging constantly.

Chapter 3

Understanding Language with Qwen 2.5

3.1 Natural Language Processing (NLP) Fundamentals

Natural Language Processing, or NLP, is a branch of Artificial Intelligence (AI) focused on enabling computers to understand, interpret, and generate human language. It's the magic behind applications like chatbots, translation services, and even your phone's autocorrect.

Why is NLP Important?

Human language is complex, filled with nuances, ambiguities, and hidden meanings. NLP aims to bridge the gap between human communication and computer understanding, making it possible for machines to:

Understand the meaning of text: Extract information, identify sentiment, and recognize entities (like people, places, and organizations).

Generate human-like text: Write stories, translate languages, and summarize documents.

Interact with humans in a natural way: Power conversational AI, like chatbots and virtual assistants.

Core Concepts in NLP:

1 Tokenization: Breaking down text into individual units (tokens), such as words, phrases, or even characters. Think of it like separating a sentence into its building blocks.

2 Part-of-Speech (POS) Tagging: Identifying the grammatical role of each word in a sentence (noun, verb, adjective, etc.). This helps the computer understand the structure and meaning of the text.

3 Named Entity Recognition (NER): Identifying and classifying named entities in text, such as people, organizations, locations, and dates. This is crucial for tasks like information extraction and knowledge graph construction.

4 Sentiment Analysis: Determining the emotional tone or attitude expressed in a piece of text (positive, negative, neutral). This is used for applications like social media monitoring and customer feedback analysis.

5 Text Summarization: Condensing a longer text into a shorter version while preserving the key information. This is useful for tasks like news summarization and document analysis.

6 Machine Translation: Converting text from one language to another. This relies on complex algorithms and vast amounts of training data to accurately capture the nuances of different languages.

NLP Techniques:

Rule-based Systems: Early NLP systems relied on handcrafted rules based on linguistic knowledge.

Statistical NLP: Uses statistical methods and machine learning algorithms to learn patterns from data.

Deep Learning: Employs deep neural networks, like Transformers, to achieve state-of-the-art results on various NLP tasks.

NLP in Everyday Life:

You encounter NLP every day, often without even realizing it!

Search Engines: Use NLP to understand your search queries and provide relevant results.

Spam Filters: Employ NLP to identify and block spam emails.

Virtual Assistants: Like Siri and Alexa, rely on NLP to understand your voice commands.

Social Media Monitoring: Uses NLP to analyze social media posts and identify trends and sentiments.

The Takeaway

NLP is a fascinating and rapidly evolving field with the potential to transform how we interact with computers and information. By understanding the fundamentals of NLP, you can appreciate the complexities of human language and the challenges and opportunities in making computers understand and generate it.

3.2 How Qwen 2.5 Processes and Understands Text

Qwen 2.5's ability to process and understand text is a marvel of modern AI. Here's a breakdown of the process, combining the power of its architecture with core NLP principles:

1. Text Input and Tokenization:

When you provide text to Qwen 2.5, it first breaks it down into smaller units called tokens. These tokens can be words, subwords, or even characters, depending on the specific tokenization method used.

This tokenization process allows Qwen 2.5 to work with the text in a structured way, similar to how we break down sentences into words to understand their meaning.

2. Embedding Representation:

Each token is then converted into a numerical representation called an embedding. This embedding captures the semantic meaning of the token, representing it as a point in a high-dimensional vector space.

Qwen 2.5 likely uses advanced embedding techniques, such as Word2Vec or Sentence-BERT, to create rich and informative embeddings that capture relationships between words and their contexts.

3. Encoder Processing:

The embeddings are then fed into the encoder, the part of Qwen 2.5's architecture responsible for understanding the input text.

The encoder consists of multiple layers of self-attention and feed-forward neural networks. These layers work together to analyze the relationships between tokens, capturing the context and meaning of the text.

Self-attention allows Qwen 2.5 to weigh the importance of different tokens in relation to each other, much like we focus on key words and phrases when understanding a sentence.

The **feed-forward networks** process the information from the attention layers, extracting further meaning and patterns.

4. Contextual Representation:

As the information flows through the encoder layers, Qwen 2.5 builds a rich contextual representation of the input text. This representation captures not only the meaning of individual words, but also their relationships and how they contribute to the overall message.

This contextual representation is key to Qwen 2.5's ability to understand nuances, ambiguities, and even humor in language.

5. Decoder Processing (for Text Generation):

If the task involves generating text, the contextual representation is passed to the decoder.

The decoder uses a similar architecture to the encoder, with self-attention and feed-forward layers.

It generates text word by word (or token by token), attending to the input representation and the previously generated text to maintain coherence and relevance.

6. Output and Interpretation:

The final output of Qwen 2.5 depends on the specific task. It could be a translation, a summary, a response to a question, or even a creative story.

The way Qwen 2.5 "understands" the text is reflected in its output. Its ability to generate relevant, coherent, and informative responses demonstrates its comprehension of the input.

Key Factors in Qwen 2.5's Understanding:

Massive Dataset: Qwen 2.5 is trained on a vast amount of text data, allowing it to learn patterns, relationships, and rules of language.

Advanced Architecture: The Transformer architecture, with its self-attention mechanism, enables Qwen 2.5 to capture complex contextual information.

Continuous Learning: Qwen 2.5 is constantly being refined and improved, incorporating new data and research findings to enhance its understanding of language.

By combining these factors, Qwen 2.5 achieves a remarkable level of text comprehension, making it a powerful tool for various NLP applications.

3.3 Sentiment Analysis, Text Summarization, and More

Beyond just understanding text, Qwen 2.5 excels at a variety of Natural Language Processing (NLP) tasks. Let's explore some of its key capabilities:

Sentiment Analysis: Decoding Emotions

Qwen 2.5 can accurately identify the sentiment expressed in a piece of text, whether it's positive, negative, or neutral. This is crucial for:

Social Media Monitoring: Understanding public opinion about a brand, product, or event by analyzing social media posts.

Customer Feedback Analysis: Gauging customer satisfaction by analyzing reviews, surveys, and support tickets.

Market Research: Identifying trends and consumer preferences by analyzing online discussions and product reviews.

Text Summarization: Getting the Gist

Qwen 2.5 can condense lengthy documents into concise summaries while preserving the key information. This is invaluable for:

News and Article Summarization: Quickly grasping the main points of news articles, research papers, or lengthy reports.

Document Analysis: Extracting key insights from legal documents, financial reports, or scientific papers.

Meeting Minutes and Reports: Automatically generating summaries of meeting discussions or project updates.

Beyond the Basics: Other NLP Capabilities

Qwen 2.5's versatility extends to other NLP tasks, including:

Question Answering: Providing accurate and relevant answers to questions posed in natural language.

Machine Translation: Translating text between multiple languages with high accuracy and fluency.

Text Generation: Creating different creative text formats, like poems, code, scripts, musical pieces, email, letters, etc.

Named Entity Recognition: Identifying and classifying named entities in text, such as people, organizations, and locations.

Topic Modeling: Discovering hidden topics and themes within a collection of documents.

How Qwen 2.5 Achieves These Capabilities

Advanced Architecture: The Transformer architecture, with its self-attention mechanism, allows Qwen 2.5 to capture complex relationships and nuances in language, which is crucial for tasks like sentiment analysis and summarization.

Massive Dataset: Training on a vast and diverse dataset enables Qwen 2.5 to learn patterns and recognize different writing styles, which is essential for tasks like text generation and translation.

Fine-tuning: Qwen 2.5 can be fine-tuned on specific datasets for different NLP tasks, optimizing its performance for those applications.

The Takeaway

Qwen 2.5's mastery of various NLP tasks makes it a powerful tool for understanding and generating human language. Its ability to analyze sentiment, summarize text, answer questions, and translate languages opens up a wide range of applications across industries, from customer service and marketing to research and education.

Chapter 4

Getting Started with Qwen 2.5

4.1 Accessing and Setting Up Qwen 2.5

1. Choose Your Access Method:

Alibaba Cloud: Qwen 2.5 is primarily hosted on Alibaba Cloud's platform. You can access it through their machine learning platform, which provides various tools and resources for working with LLMs. This is generally a good option for those who need robust infrastructure and support.

Hugging Face: Some versions of Qwen 2.5 are available on Hugging Face Model Hub. This is a popular platform for accessing and sharing pre-trained models. This can be a more accessible option for individual developers and researchers.

Local Installation (For Developers): If you have the necessary hardware and expertise, you can potentially download and install Qwen 2.5 locally. However, this requires significant computational resources and technical knowledge.

2. Create an Account and Configure Access:

Alibaba Cloud: If you're using Alibaba Cloud, you'll need to create an account and configure your access to their machine learning platform. This may involve setting up API keys and configuring your development environment.

Hugging Face: Create an account on Hugging Face and familiarize yourself with their platform and tools.

3. Choose Your Qwen 2.5 Model:

Qwen 2.5 comes in different sizes and variations, each with its own strengths and resource requirements. Consider your needs and available resources when choosing a model.

Smaller models: Suitable for tasks with less demanding computational needs or if you have limited resources.

Larger models: Offer higher performance and capabilities but require more powerful hardware.

4. Set Up Your Development Environment:

Programming Language: Qwen 2.5 typically supports Python, a popular language for machine learning and AI development. Make sure you have a compatible Python environment set up.

Libraries and Frameworks: You'll need to install the necessary libraries and frameworks for working with LLMs, such as Transformers (Hugging Face) or Alibaba Cloud's SDKs.

Hardware: Ensure your hardware meets the requirements of the chosen Qwen 2.5 model. Larger models may require powerful GPUs or TPUs for optimal performance.

5. Start Experimenting!

Once your environment is set up, you can start experimenting with Qwen 2.5! Explore its capabilities through various tasks, such as text generation, translation, question answering, and code generation.

Refer to Documentation: Alibaba Cloud and Hugging Face provide documentation and examples to help you get started.

Tips for Accessing and Setting Up Qwen 2.5:

Start with a Smaller Model: If you're new to LLMs, start with a smaller Qwen 2.5 model to get familiar with the process and avoid overwhelming your resources.

Explore Tutorials and Examples: Alibaba Cloud and Hugging Face offer tutorials and examples to guide you through the setup process and demonstrate various use cases.

Join the Community: Engage with the Qwen 2.5 community on forums and online platforms to learn from others and get support.

By following these steps and utilizing the available resources, you can successfully access and set up Qwen 2.5 to unlock its powerful capabilities for your projects and applications.

4.2 API Basics and Key Functions

APIs (Application Programming Interfaces) are the bridges that allow different software systems to communicate and interact with each other. Qwen 2.5, like many other advanced AI models, is accessible through an API, enabling developers to integrate its capabilities into their applications.

What is an API?

Imagine an API as a waiter in a restaurant. You (the application) give the waiter (the API) your order (a request), and the waiter relays it to the kitchen (the AI model). The kitchen prepares your food (processes the request) and sends it back through the waiter (the API) to you (the application).

Key Concepts in APIs:

Request: This is what you send to the API, specifying the task you want the AI model to perform (e.g., generate text, translate a sentence, answer a question).

Response: This is what the API sends back to you, containing the results of the AI model's processing (e.g., generated text, translated sentence, answer to the question).

Endpoint: This is the specific URL you send your request to. Different endpoints may be available for different tasks or functionalities.

Authentication: This is the process of verifying your identity to ensure you have permission to access the API. This often involves API keys or tokens.

Key Functions of the Qwen 2.5 API:

Text Generation: Generate creative and informative text formats, like poems, code, scripts, musical pieces, email, letters, etc.

Text Completion: Complete a given text prompt, generating the next word, sentence, or paragraph.

Question Answering: Provide answers to questions posed in natural language.

Language Translation: Translate text between multiple languages.

Code Generation: Generate code in various programming languages.

Summarization: Condense lengthy documents into concise summaries.

Sentiment Analysis: Analyze the sentiment expressed in a piece of text.

Using the Qwen 2.5 API:

1 Obtain API Credentials: You'll need to obtain API credentials, such as an API key or token, to authenticate your requests.

2 Construct Your Request: Formulate your request according to the API's specifications, including the endpoint, parameters, and data.

3 Send the Request: Use a programming language like Python to send your request to the API endpoint.

4 Process the Response: Parse the API's response to extract the information or results you need.

Example Code Snippet (Python):

Python

```python
import requests

api_key = "YOUR_API_KEY"
endpoint = "https://qwen-api.alibaba.com/generate_text"

prompt = "Write a short story about a cat who goes on an adventure."

headers = {
  "Authorization": f"Bearer {api_key}"
}

data = {
  "prompt": prompt
}

response = requests.post(endpoint, headers=headers, json=data)

if response.status_code == 200:
  story = response.json()["generated_text"]
```

```
  print(story)
else:
  print(f"Error: {response.status_code}")
```

Benefits of Using the API:

Easy Integration: Integrate Qwen 2.5's capabilities into your applications without needing to manage the underlying infrastructure.

Scalability: Scale your usage based on your needs, from small-scale experiments to large-scale deployments.

Accessibility: Access Qwen 2.5 from anywhere with an internet connection.

Flexibility: Use your preferred programming language and tools to interact with the API.

By understanding the basics of APIs and the key functions of the Qwen 2.5 API, you can leverage its powerful capabilities to build innovative and intelligent applications.

4.3 Your First Qwen 2.5 Project

It's time to put your Qwen 2.5 knowledge into action! Here's a simple project to get you started, assuming you've set up your access and development environment as described in the previous sections:

Project: A Qwen 2.5-Powered "Idea Generator"

This project will use Qwen 2.5 to generate creative ideas based on user prompts. It's a great way to explore the text generation capabilities of the model.

1. Define the Task:

The goal is to create a simple program that takes a user prompt as input (e.g., "ideas for a birthday party," "creative business ideas," "story ideas about a talking dog") and uses Qwen 2.5 to generate a list of ideas.

2. Choose Your API:

Decide whether you'll use the Alibaba Cloud API or access Qwen 2.5 through Hugging Face. Refer to the previous section on API basics if needed.

3. Write the Code:

Here's a basic Python code example using the hypothetical Qwen 2.5 API (adapt it based on your chosen access method):

Python

```
import requests


api_key = "YOUR_API_KEY"   # Replace with your
actual API key
endpoint =
"https://qwen-api.alibaba.com/generate_text"   #
Replace with the actual endpoint


def generate_ideas(prompt):
  headers = {
    "Authorization": f"Bearer {api_key}"
  }

  data = {
```

```python
        "prompt": f"Generate creative ideas for: {prompt}",
        "max_tokens": 100  # Adjust as needed
    }

    response = requests.post(endpoint, headers=headers, json=data)

    if response.status_code == 200:
        ideas = response.json()["generated_text"]
        return ideas
    else:
        return f"Error: {response.status_code}"

# Get user input
user_prompt = input("Enter a topic for idea generation: ")

# Generate ideas
ideas = generate_ideas(user_prompt)

# Print the results
print("\nHere are some ideas:")
print(ideas)
```

4. Run and Test:

Execute your code and test it with different prompts. Observe how Qwen 2.5 generates creative and relevant ideas based on your input.

5. Enhance Your Project:

Improve User Interface: Instead of a basic command-line interface, create a more user-friendly interface using libraries like Tkinter or PyQt.

Add Refinement Options: Allow users to refine the generated ideas by providing additional prompts or specifying the number of ideas they want.

Incorporate Other NLP Tasks: Combine idea generation with other Qwen 2.5 capabilities, such as sentiment analysis to evaluate the generated ideas or summarization to provide concise descriptions.

Key Takeaways:

This project provides a hands-on experience with using the Qwen 2.5 API for text generation.

It demonstrates how to interact with the API, send requests, and process responses.

It encourages experimentation and creativity in exploring the capabilities of Qwen 2.5.

By starting with this simple project, you can gain confidence in using Qwen 2.5 and pave the way for more complex and ambitious applications. Remember to refer to the API documentation and explore the available resources to further enhance your project and unlock the full potential of Qwen 2.5.

Chapter 5

Fine-tuning Qwen 2.5

5.1 Customizing Qwen 2.5 for Specific Tasks

While Qwen 2.5 is powerful out-of-the-box, fine-tuning allows you to tailor it to excel in specific tasks and domains. Think of it like taking a talented athlete and providing specialized training to become a champion in a particular sport.

Why Fine-Tune?

Improved Accuracy: Fine-tuning helps Qwen 2.5 learn the nuances of your specific task, leading to more accurate and relevant outputs.

Enhanced Efficiency: A fine-tuned model can often achieve better results with less input, making it more efficient for your application.

Domain Adaptation: Fine-tuning allows you to adapt Qwen 2.5 to your specific domain or industry, improving its understanding of specialized terminology and context.

Reduced Bias: Fine-tuning can help mitigate biases present in the pre-trained model, ensuring fairer and more appropriate responses.

The Fine-Tuning Process:

1 Gather Task-Specific Data: Collect a dataset of examples that represent the task you want Qwen 2.5 to perform. For example, if you're fine-tuning for customer service, gather conversations between customers and support agents.

2 Prepare the Data: Clean and format your data to make it suitable for training. This may involve removing irrelevant information, labeling examples, and converting data into a compatible format.

3 Select a Fine-Tuning Method:

Full Fine-Tuning: Update all of the model's parameters. This is resource-intensive but can lead to significant performance improvements.

Parameter-Efficient Fine-Tuning (PEFT): Update only a small subset of parameters, making the process more efficient. Popular PEFT techniques include LoRA (Low-Rank Adaptation) and prompt tuning.

4 Train the Model: Use your prepared data to train Qwen 2.5, adjusting its parameters to optimize performance on the specific task. This involves feeding the data to the model and using an optimization algorithm to minimize errors.

5 Evaluate Performance: Assess the performance of the fine-tuned model on a separate dataset to ensure it generalizes well to unseen data.

6 Deploy and Monitor: Deploy your fine-tuned Qwen 2.5 model in your application and monitor its performance over time. You may need to retrain or adjust the model as new data becomes available or requirements change.

Example: Fine-Tuning for Code Generation

Let's say you want Qwen 2.5 to generate Python code for specific data analysis tasks. You could fine-tune it on a dataset of Python code snippets along with corresponding descriptions of the tasks they perform. This would allow Qwen 2.5 to learn the patterns and conventions of Python code for data analysis, improving its ability to generate accurate and efficient code for similar tasks.

Tools and Resources:

Alibaba Cloud: Provides tools and resources for fine-tuning Qwen 2.5 on their platform.

Hugging Face: Offers libraries like Transformers and Accelerate, which can be used for fine-tuning LLMs.

PEFT Libraries: Explore libraries like `peft` and `bitsandbytes` for implementing parameter-efficient fine-tuning techniques.

Key Takeaways:

Fine-tuning is crucial for customizing Qwen 2.5 to excel in specific tasks and domains.

Choose the appropriate fine-tuning method based on your needs and resources.

Carefully prepare your data and evaluate the performance of your fine-tuned model.

By mastering the art of fine-tuning, you can unlock the full potential of Qwen 2.5 and create AI applications that are truly tailored to your needs.

5.2 Data Preparation and Training Techniques

Fine-tuning Qwen 2.5 effectively hinges on proper data preparation and the right training techniques. Let's delve into the essential steps:

1. Data Preparation: The Foundation

Gather Task-Specific Data:

Relevance is Key: Your data must align with the specific task you want Qwen 2.5 to perform. For example, if you're fine-tuning for writing creative stories, your dataset should consist of diverse examples of stories.

Diversity Matters: Include a wide range of examples to ensure the model generalizes well and avoids biases.

Consider Data Sources: Explore books, articles, websites, code repositories, and even create your own data if needed.

Clean and Preprocess the Data:

Handle Noise: Remove irrelevant information, errors, and inconsistencies.

Format for Consistency: Ensure data is in a consistent format that Qwen 2.5 can understand (e.g., text files, JSON, CSV).

Tokenization: Consider the tokenization method used by Qwen 2.5 and ensure your data is tokenized accordingly.

Format for Fine-tuning:

Input-Output Pairs: Structure your data as input-output pairs. For example, if you're fine-tuning for question answering, each pair would be a question and its corresponding answer.

Special Tokens: Use special tokens to indicate the beginning and end of sequences or to separate different parts of the input.

2. Training Techniques: Shaping the Model

Choose a Fine-Tuning Method:

Full Fine-tuning: Update all parameters, resource-intensive but potentially very effective.

Parameter-Efficient Fine-Tuning (PEFT): Update a smaller subset of parameters, more efficient but may have limitations. Consider techniques like LoRA, prompt tuning, or adapter modules.

Optimization Algorithms:

AdamW: A popular optimization algorithm for fine-tuning LLMs. It adapts the learning rate for each parameter, leading to faster and more stable convergence.

Hyperparameter Tuning:

Learning Rate: Controls how much the model's parameters are adjusted during training.

Batch Size: The number of examples processed in each training iteration.

Epochs: The number of times the entire training dataset is passed through the model.

Experiment and Evaluate: Find the optimal hyperparameter values for your specific task and dataset through experimentation and careful evaluation.

Regularization Techniques:

Dropout: Randomly drop out some neurons during training to prevent overfitting.

Weight Decay: Add a penalty to large weights to prevent the model from becoming too complex and overfitting the training data.

Early Stopping: Monitor the model's performance on a validation set and stop training when performance starts to decrease to prevent overfitting.

3. Evaluation: Measuring Success

Metrics:

Accuracy, Precision, Recall, F1-score: For classification tasks.

BLEU, ROUGE: For text generation and summarization tasks.

Perplexity: Measures how well the model predicts the next token in a sequence.

Split Data: Divide your data into training, validation, and test sets. Use the training set for training, the validation set for hyperparameter tuning and early stopping, and the test set for final evaluation.

Key Considerations:

Computational Resources: Fine-tuning large models requires significant computational power. Consider using cloud platforms or specialized hardware.

Data Quality: The quality of your data is crucial for successful fine-tuning. Ensure your data is relevant, diverse, and properly cleaned.

Experimentation: Fine-tuning is an iterative process. Experiment with different techniques, hyperparameters, and data to achieve optimal results.

By following these data preparation and training techniques, you can effectively fine-tune Qwen 2.5 to excel in your specific tasks and create powerful AI applications.

5.3 Optimizing Performance and Efficiency

Fine-tuning Qwen 2.5 is just the first step. To truly unleash its power, you need to optimize its performance and efficiency. This involves a combination of techniques and strategies to ensure it runs smoothly, generates high-quality outputs, and minimizes resource consumption.

1. Hardware Optimization:

GPU Acceleration: Utilize powerful GPUs or TPUs to accelerate the computationally intensive tasks involved in running Qwen 2.5.

Memory Management: Optimize memory allocation and usage to avoid bottlenecks and ensure smooth processing.

Distributed Training: For large-scale fine-tuning, consider using distributed training techniques to spread the workload across multiple GPUs or machines.

2. Model Optimization:

Quantization: Reduce the precision of the model's parameters (e.g., from 32-bit floating point to 16-bit or even 8-bit integers). This can significantly reduce memory footprint and improve inference speed with minimal impact on accuracy.

Pruning: Remove less important connections or neurons in the model to reduce its size and complexity.

Knowledge Distillation: Train a smaller "student" model to mimic the behavior of the larger Qwen 2.5 model. This can result in a more compact and efficient model with comparable performance.

3. Software Optimization:

Efficient Code: Write clean and optimized code for interacting with the Qwen 2.5 API and processing its outputs.

Caching: Cache frequently used data or computations to avoid redundant processing.

Batching: Process multiple requests in batches to improve throughput and reduce overhead.

Asynchronous Operations: Utilize asynchronous operations to avoid blocking and improve responsiveness.

4. Hyperparameter Tuning:

Fine-tune hyperparameters: Experiment with different hyperparameter values, such as learning rate, batch size, and sequence length, to find the optimal settings for your specific task and hardware.

Optimization Algorithms: Explore different optimization algorithms, such as AdamW or SGD, to find the one that converges fastest and achieves the best performance.

5. Monitoring and Analysis:

Performance Metrics: Continuously monitor key performance metrics, such as inference speed, memory usage, and accuracy, to identify potential bottlenecks or areas for improvement.

Profiling Tools: Use profiling tools to analyze the performance of your code and identify areas where optimizations can be made.

6. Stay Updated:

New Techniques: Keep abreast of the latest research and advancements in LLM optimization. New techniques and tools are constantly being developed.

Qwen 2.5 Updates: Stay informed about updates and improvements to Qwen 2.5 itself, as these may include performance enhancements or new optimization options.

Key Takeaways:

Optimizing performance and efficiency is crucial for deploying Qwen 2.5 effectively in real-world applications.

Consider a holistic approach, combining hardware, model, and software optimizations.

Continuously monitor and analyze performance to identify areas for improvement.

By implementing these optimization strategies, you can ensure that Qwen 2.5 runs smoothly, delivers high-quality results, and maximizes the return on your investment in this powerful AI technology.

Chapter 6

Building Applications with Qwen 2.5

6.1 Developing Chatbots and Conversational AI

Qwen 2.5's advanced language capabilities make it a perfect foundation for building sophisticated chatbots and conversational AI systems. These systems can engage in human-like conversations, understand user intent, and provide helpful and informative responses.

1. Design the Conversation Flow:

Define Purpose and Scope: Determine the primary goal of your chatbot. What tasks should it perform? What topics should it be knowledgeable about?

Create a Conversational Structure: Map out potential user inputs and corresponding chatbot responses. Consider different conversation paths and how the chatbot should handle unexpected inputs.

Maintain Context: Ensure the chatbot remembers previous interactions and maintains context throughout the conversation. This creates a more natural and engaging experience.

2. Leverage Qwen 2.5's Capabilities:

Text Generation: Use Qwen 2.5 to generate human-like responses that are relevant to the conversation and user input.

Question Answering: Utilize Qwen 2.5's question-answering abilities to provide accurate and informative responses to user queries.

Sentiment Analysis: Incorporate sentiment analysis to understand the user's emotional state and tailor the chatbot's responses accordingly.

Multi-turn Conversations: Leverage Qwen 2.5's large context window to handle multi-turn conversations and maintain a consistent understanding of the dialogue.

3. Enhance the Chatbot's Personality:

Define a Persona: Give your chatbot a distinct personality that aligns with its purpose and target audience. This could include a name, backstory, and communication style.

Inject Humor and Emotion: Use Qwen 2.5's creative writing capabilities to add humor, empathy, and other emotions to the chatbot's responses.

Adapt to User Preferences: Personalize the chatbot's responses based on user preferences and past interactions.

4. Integrate with Other Systems:

Connect to Data Sources: Integrate the chatbot with external data sources, such as knowledge bases, databases, or APIs, to provide accurate and up-to-date information.

Connect to Services: Enable the chatbot to perform actions or access services, such as booking appointments, making reservations, or providing customer support.

5. Test and Refine:

Conduct Thorough Testing: Test the chatbot with various user inputs and scenarios to identify potential issues or areas for improvement.

Gather User Feedback: Collect feedback from users to understand their experience and identify areas where the chatbot can be enhanced.

Iterate and Improve: Continuously refine the chatbot's conversation flow, responses, and personality based on testing and feedback.

Example Use Cases:

Customer Service: Provide 24/7 support, answer frequently asked questions, and resolve customer issues.

E-commerce: Guide customers through product selection, provide personalized recommendations, and assist with purchases.

Education: Offer interactive learning experiences, provide personalized feedback, and answer student questions.

Healthcare: Provide basic medical information, schedule appointments, and offer emotional support.

Tools and Resources:

Alibaba Cloud: Offers tools and platforms for building and deploying chatbots.

Hugging Face: Provides libraries and models for conversational AI development.

Dialogflow (Google): A platform for building conversational interfaces.

Rasa: An open-source framework for conversational AI.

By combining Qwen 2.5's powerful language capabilities with thoughtful design and development, you can create engaging and helpful chatbots that enhance user experiences and transform interactions.

6.2 Content Generation and Creative Writing

Qwen 2.5 isn't just about answering questions and summarizing text; it's also a powerful tool for content generation and creative writing. Unleash your imagination and let Qwen 2.5 be your muse!

1. Explore Different Content Formats:

Stories: Generate short stories, novels, or even screenplays with compelling plots, engaging characters, and vivid descriptions.

Poems: Compose poems in various styles, from sonnets and haikus to free verse, exploring different themes and emotions.

Scripts: Create scripts for plays, movies, or even video games, with engaging dialogue and dramatic tension.

Articles and Blog Posts: Generate informative and engaging articles or blog posts on a variety of topics.

Marketing Copy: Craft compelling ad copy, product descriptions, or social media posts that capture attention and drive conversions.

2. Provide Creative Prompts:

Spark Inspiration: Give Qwen 2.5 a starting point, such as a title, a character description, or a plot idea, and let it generate the rest.

Experiment with Styles: Ask Qwen 2.5 to write in a specific style, such as "a mystery story in the style of Agatha Christie" or "a poem in the style of Shakespeare."

Set Constraints: Challenge Qwen 2.5 with constraints, such as "write a story in exactly 100 words" or "write a poem that rhymes every other line."

3. Refine and Iterate:

Edit and Refine: Use Qwen 2.5's output as a starting point and refine it with your own creativity and editing skills.

Collaborate with Qwen 2.5: Engage in a back-and-forth process with Qwen 2.5, providing feedback and refining its output until you achieve the desired result.

Experiment with Different Prompts: Try different prompts and parameters to explore the full range of Qwen 2.5's creative potential.

4. Overcome Writer's Block:

Generate Ideas: Use Qwen 2.5 to brainstorm ideas when you're feeling stuck.

Explore New Perspectives: Ask Qwen 2.5 to generate different versions of a scene or story to gain new perspectives.

Spark Creativity: Use Qwen 2.5's unexpected outputs as a springboard for your own ideas.

5. Ethical Considerations:

Originality and Plagiarism: While Qwen 2.5 can generate creative content, it's important to ensure originality and avoid plagiarism. Use its output as inspiration or a starting point, but add your own unique voice and ideas.

Bias and Sensitivity: Be mindful of potential biases in the generated content and ensure it aligns with ethical and social standards.

Examples:

Generate a children's story about a magical unicorn who befriends a lonely child.

Write a poem about the beauty of nature in the style of William Wordsworth.

Create a script for a short film about a time traveler who gets stuck in the past.

Generate marketing copy for a new smartphone that emphasizes its innovative features.

Tools and Resources:

Alibaba Cloud: Provides tools and platforms for content generation.

Hugging Face: Offers models and libraries for creative writing.

AI Dungeon: A text-based adventure game powered by AI.

Sudowrite: An AI writing assistant that helps with creative writing tasks.

By embracing Qwen 2.5's creative potential and combining it with your own imagination, you can unlock new levels of storytelling, poetry, and content creation. Let Qwen 2.5 be your partner in bringing your creative visions to life.

6.3 Integrating Qwen 2.5 into Existing Systems

Qwen 2.5's power isn't limited to standalone applications. You can seamlessly integrate it into your existing systems to enhance their functionality and intelligence. This opens up a world of possibilities for improving workflows, automating tasks, and creating more intelligent user experiences.

1. Identify Integration Points:

Analyze your systems: Identify areas where Qwen 2.5's capabilities can add value. This could include customer service platforms, content management systems, data analysis tools, or even internal communication channels.

Consider user needs: Think about how Qwen 2.5 can improve user experiences within your existing systems. Can it provide better search results, offer personalized recommendations, or automate repetitive tasks?

2. Choose the Right Integration Method:

API Integration: The most common approach, using the Qwen 2.5 API to send requests and receive responses within your existing system. This allows for flexibility and scalability.

Direct Integration: For more advanced use cases, consider directly integrating Qwen 2.5 into your system's codebase. This may require more technical expertise but can offer greater control and customization.

Hybrid Approach: Combine API integration with direct integration for specific functionalities or modules.

3. Data Flow and Transformation:

Ensure Compatibility: Ensure that data flowing between your existing system and Qwen 2.5 is compatible in terms of format, encoding, and structure.

Data Transformation: Implement data transformation processes to convert data into a format that Qwen 2.5 can understand and utilize.

Data Security: Implement appropriate security measures to protect sensitive data during transfer and processing.

4. User Interface and Experience:

Seamless Integration: Integrate Qwen 2.5's functionalities into the user interface of your existing system in a way that feels natural and intuitive.

Clear Communication: Provide clear instructions and feedback to users when interacting with Qwen 2.5-powered features.

Personalization: Use Qwen 2.5 to personalize user experiences within your existing system, such as providing tailored recommendations or adapting to user preferences.

5. Testing and Monitoring:

Thorough Testing: Test the integration thoroughly to ensure it functions as expected and doesn't disrupt existing workflows.

Performance Monitoring: Monitor the performance of the integrated system to identify potential bottlenecks or areas for optimization.

User Feedback: Gather user feedback to understand their experience with the integrated Qwen 2.5 functionalities and identify areas for improvement.

Example Use Cases:

Enhance a Customer Support Platform: Integrate Qwen 2.5 to provide instant answers to common questions, automate ticket routing, and personalize support interactions.

Improve a Content Management System: Use Qwen 2.5 to generate content ideas, assist with writing and editing, and personalize content recommendations.

Boost a Data Analysis Tool: Integrate Qwen 2.5 to analyze data, generate reports, and provide insights in natural language.

Power an Internal Communication Tool: Use Qwen 2.5 to summarize conversations, translate messages, and assist with scheduling and task management.

Key Takeaways:

Integrating Qwen 2.5 into existing systems can significantly enhance their functionality and intelligence.

Choose the right integration method based on your needs and technical expertise.

Ensure data compatibility, user experience, and thorough testing for successful integration.

By thoughtfully integrating Qwen 2.5 into your existing systems, you can unlock new levels of efficiency, automation, and user satisfaction.

Chapter 7

Prompt Engineering for Qwen 2.5

7.1 Crafting Effective Prompts for Optimal Results

Crafting effective prompts is crucial for getting the most out of large language models like Qwen 2.5. Here's a breakdown of how to write prompts that yield optimal results:

1. Be Clear and Specific:

Define your task explicitly: Clearly state what you want the model to do (e.g., "Summarize this article," "Translate this text into French," "Write a poem about nature").

Provide context: Give the model the necessary background information to understand your request (e.g., "Given the following facts about the American Revolution...").

Specify the desired output: Indicate the format, length, or style you expect (e.g., "Write a short story in the style of Edgar Allan Poe," "Generate a list of bullet points").

2. Use Keywords and Constraints:

Incorporate relevant keywords: Help the model focus on the key concepts and topics.

Set constraints: Guide the model by specifying limitations or requirements (e.g., "Write a tweet with no more than 280 characters," "Generate a code snippet in Python").

3. Structure for Clarity:

Use clear and concise language: Avoid ambiguity and complex sentence structures.

Break down complex tasks: Divide a complex request into smaller, more manageable subtasks.

Organize information logically: Present information in a structured way, using headings, bullet points, or numbered lists.

4. Experiment and Iterate:

Start with simple prompts: Gradually increase complexity as you become more familiar with the model's capabilities.

Try different approaches: Experiment with various phrasing, keywords, and constraints to see what works best.

Refine your prompts: Analyze the model's output and adjust your prompts accordingly to improve the results.

5. Advanced Techniques:

Few-shot learning: Provide a few examples of the desired output to guide the model.

Chain-of-thought prompting: Encourage the model to reason step-by-step by including phrases like "Let's think step by step."

Prompt engineering frameworks: Explore frameworks like "PromptChainer" to manage and optimize complex prompts.

Examples:

Ineffective prompt: "Write something about space."

Effective prompt: "Write a short story about an astronaut who discovers a new form of life on a distant planet. The story should be written in a suspenseful tone and have a surprising twist ending."

By following these guidelines and practicing your prompt engineering skills, you can effectively guide Qwen 2.5 to generate high-quality output that meets your specific needs.

7.2 Advanced Prompting Techniques and Strategies

You're diving into the exciting world of advanced prompting! This is where we move beyond basic instructions and explore techniques to truly unlock the potential of large language models like Qwen 2.5. Here's a breakdown of some powerful strategies:

1. Few-Shot Learning:

Concept: Instead of just giving a task, provide a few examples of the desired input-output pairs. This helps the model understand the pattern and generalize better.

Example:

Prompt: "Translate these English phrases to Spanish:

Hello: Hola

Good morning: Buenos días

How are you?: ¿Cómo estás?

Now translate: Thank you"

Expected Output: Gracias

2. Chain-of-Thought Prompting:

Concept: Encourage the model to break down complex reasoning tasks into intermediate steps, mimicking human thought processes. This leads to more accurate and logical outputs.

Example:

Prompt: "Roger has 5 tennis balls. He buys 2 more cans of tennis balls. Each can has 3 tennis balls. How many tennis balls does Roger have now? Let's think step by step."

Expected Output:

Step 1: Roger starts with 5 balls.

Step 2: He buys 2 cans * 3 balls/can = 6 balls.

Step 3: Roger has 5 + 6 = 11 balls. **Answer:** Roger has 11 tennis balls.

3. Self-Consistency:

Concept: For tasks with multiple valid solutions, generate multiple outputs using different prompts or variations. Then, select the most frequent or consistent answer. This improves reliability.

Example: Useful for tasks like common sense reasoning or multiple-choice questions where the model might initially give varying answers.

4. Generated Knowledge Prompting:

Concept: Instead of relying solely on the model's internal knowledge, use the model itself to generate relevant information or context before asking the main question.

Example:

Prompt:

1 "Write a short paragraph about the history of the internet."

2 "(Model generates paragraph about the internet)"

3 "Based on the above paragraph, what was a key factor in the internet's rapid growth?"

5. ReAct (Reason + Act):

Concept: Combine reasoning and action in a loop, especially useful for tasks involving external information or tools. The model reasons about what to do, takes an action (like a Google search), and then uses the result to reason further.

Example: "I want to find a recipe for chocolate chip cookies without nuts. First, search for recipes." (The model would then use a search tool and refine the search based on the results until it finds a suitable recipe).

Important Notes:

Experimentation is key: These techniques are not one-size-fits-all. Try different variations and combinations to find what works best for your specific task and the Qwen 2.5 model you're using.

Prompt engineering is iterative: Analyze the model's output and refine your prompts based on the results.

Consider the model's limitations: Even with advanced techniques, large language models have limitations. Be mindful of potential biases and inaccuracies.

By mastering these advanced prompting techniques, you can significantly enhance the quality and reliability of the outputs you get from Qwen 2.5, enabling you to tackle more complex and nuanced tasks.

7.3 Prompt Engineering for Different Applications

Prompt engineering is like giving directions to a highly capable but somewhat literal-minded assistant. The better your directions, the better the outcome. Here's how to tailor your prompts for specific applications:

1. Content Creation:

Goal: Generate creative text formats like articles, stories, poems, scripts, etc.

Prompt strategies:

Define the genre, style, and tone: "Write a short story in the style of Agatha Christie, with a mysterious tone and a surprising twist ending."

Provide a detailed outline or plot points: "Write a screenplay about a time traveler who meets their younger self. Include scenes in their childhood, their present life as a scientist, and a dramatic confrontation in the future."

Specify character details and relationships: "Write a romantic comedy about two rival chefs who are forced to work together on a cooking competition show. The female lead is ambitious and driven, while the male lead is laid-back and charming."

Use evocative language and imagery: "Write a poem about the feeling of nostalgia, using metaphors related to fading photographs and forgotten melodies."

2. Code Generation:

Goal: Generate code snippets, complete functions, or translate between programming languages.

Prompt strategies:

Specify the programming language and desired functionality: "Write a Python function to sort a list of numbers in descending order."

Provide code context and comments: "/* This function should calculate the factorial of a given number */ function factorial(n) { // Complete this function }"

Use examples and test cases: "Write a JavaScript function to validate an email address. Here are some examples of valid and invalid email formats:"

Describe the desired output or behavior: "Generate a C++ program that simulates a simple calculator with addition, subtraction, multiplication, and division operations."

3. Data Analysis and Knowledge Retrieval:

Goal: Extract insights from data, answer questions based on provided information, or summarize complex topics.

Prompt strategies:

Clearly define the task and scope: "Analyze this dataset of customer reviews and identify the top three reasons for customer dissatisfaction."

Structure the input data: "Given the following table of sales data, calculate the average monthly revenue for the year 2023."

Specify the desired output format: "Summarize the key findings of this scientific article in a bullet-point list."

Use precise language and avoid ambiguity: "What were the main causes of the French Revolution? Provide a concise answer with historical evidence."

4. Translation:

Goal: Translate text between different languages.

Prompt strategies:

Clearly indicate the source and target languages: "Translate this paragraph from English to Japanese."

Provide context for ambiguous phrases: "Translate 'bank' in the context of a river."

Specify the desired level of formality: "Translate this business letter into formal German."

5. Chatbots and Conversational AI:

Goal: Create engaging and informative conversational experiences.

Prompt strategies:

Define the chatbot's persona and purpose: "You are a friendly and helpful customer support agent for an online bookstore."

Provide example conversations: "Here are some examples of how the chatbot should interact with users:"

Specify topics and areas of expertise: "The chatbot should be knowledgeable about different book genres, authors, and current bestsellers."

Use natural language and open-ended questions: "How can I help you today?"

Remember to adapt these strategies to the specific capabilities of Qwen 2.5 and your chosen application. By carefully crafting your prompts, you can effectively guide the model to generate high-quality output that meets your needs.

Chapter 8

Ethical Considerations and Responsible AI

8.1 Bias, Fairness, and Transparency in LLMs

You've hit on a crucial aspect of LLMs like Qwen 2.5! Bias, fairness, and transparency are essential considerations for responsible development and deployment. Here's a breakdown:

1. Understanding Bias in LLMs:

Source of Bias: LLMs learn from massive datasets of text and code, which often contain societal biases, stereotypes, and discriminatory language. This can lead to models reflecting and even amplifying these biases in their output.

Types of Bias:

Gender bias: Associating certain roles or characteristics with specific genders.

Racial and ethnic bias: Perpetuating stereotypes or exhibiting prejudice towards certain groups.

Cultural bias: Favoring or misunderstanding certain cultural perspectives.

Socioeconomic bias: Discriminating based on economic status or social class.

2. Why Fairness Matters:

Ethical Considerations: Biased LLMs can perpetuate harmful stereotypes and discrimination, leading to unfair or unequal treatment of individuals and groups.

Trust and Acceptance: Users need to trust that LLMs are fair and unbiased to confidently use them in various applications.

Social Impact: Biased LLMs can have negative consequences on society, reinforcing existing inequalities and hindering progress towards a more just and equitable world.

3. Promoting Transparency:

Data and Training: Be transparent about the data used to train LLMs, including its source, size, and potential biases.

Model Architecture: Provide clear explanations of how the model works, its limitations, and potential sources of bias.

Evaluation and Metrics: Use diverse and representative evaluation datasets to assess bias and fairness. Develop metrics that specifically measure bias in different forms.

Explainability: Strive to make the model's decision-making process more transparent and understandable to users.

4. Mitigating Bias:

Data Curation: Carefully curate training data to reduce bias and ensure representation of diverse perspectives.

Bias Detection and Correction: Develop techniques to detect and mitigate bias in both training data and model outputs.

Adversarial Training: Train models to be robust to biased inputs and avoid generating discriminatory outputs.

Human Oversight: Incorporate human review and feedback in the development and deployment process.

5. Qwen 2.5 and Bias:

While Qwen 2.5 has likely been trained on a massive dataset, it's important to be aware of the potential for bias in its outputs. Here's what you can do:

Critical Evaluation: Carefully evaluate the model's responses for any signs of bias, especially in sensitive applications.

Prompt Engineering: Design prompts that encourage fair and unbiased responses.

Feedback and Reporting: Provide feedback to the developers if you encounter biased outputs.

By actively addressing bias, fairness, and transparency, we can ensure that LLMs like Qwen 2.5 are used responsibly and ethically, contributing to a more just and inclusive society.

8.2 Addressing Potential Risks and Challenges

You're right to be thinking about the potential risks and challenges! While LLMs like Qwen 2.5 offer incredible potential, it's important to approach them with awareness and a plan to mitigate potential downsides. Here are some key areas to consider:

1. Misinformation and Manipulation:

Challenge: LLMs can be used to generate convincing but false information, potentially spreading propaganda, fake news, or creating deepfakes.

Mitigation:

Develop detection mechanisms: Invest in tools and techniques to identify AI-generated content and flag potential misinformation.

Promote media literacy: Educate users on how to critically evaluate information and identify potential manipulation.

Responsible generation: Build safeguards into LLMs to prevent the generation of harmful or misleading content.

2. Job Displacement and Economic Impact:

Challenge: LLMs could automate tasks previously performed by humans, potentially leading to job displacement in certain sectors.

Mitigation:

Focus on augmentation: Emphasize how LLMs can augment human capabilities rather than replace them entirely.

Reskilling and upskilling: Invest in programs to help workers adapt to new roles and acquire skills relevant to AI technologies.

Ethical considerations: Consider the societal impact of LLM deployment and ensure fair transitions for workers.

3. Privacy and Security:

Challenge: LLMs can be used to generate sensitive or private information, potentially violating individual privacy or exposing confidential data.

Mitigation:

Data anonymization: Implement techniques to anonymize and protect sensitive data used in training and deployment.

Access control: Restrict access to LLMs and their outputs to authorized users.

Security measures: Implement robust security protocols to prevent unauthorized access and misuse of LLMs.

4. Ethical Concerns and Bias:

Challenge: As mentioned earlier, LLMs can reflect and amplify biases present in their training data, leading to unfair or discriminatory outcomes.

Mitigation:

Bias detection and mitigation: Develop methods to identify and mitigate bias in both training data and model outputs.

Ethical guidelines: Establish clear ethical guidelines for LLM development and deployment.

Diverse perspectives: Involve diverse stakeholders in the development process to ensure inclusivity and fairness.

5. Overreliance and Deskilling:

Challenge: Overreliance on LLMs could lead to a decline in critical thinking and problem-solving skills in humans.

Mitigation:

Promote human oversight: Ensure human review and validation of LLM outputs, especially in critical applications.

Education and awareness: Educate users about the limitations of LLMs and the importance of human judgment.

Balanced approach: Encourage a balanced approach that combines the strengths of both humans and AI.

Addressing these risks and challenges requires a multi-faceted approach involving researchers, developers, policymakers, and the public. By proactively addressing these concerns, we can harness the transformative potential of LLMs like Qwen 2.5 while mitigating their potential negative impacts.

8.3 Guidelines for Ethical AI Development

You're spot on in recognizing the importance of ethical considerations in AI development. Here's a framework of guidelines to ensure responsible AI:

1. Human-Centered Design:

Prioritize human well-being: AI systems should be designed to serve humanity and promote societal good. Consider the potential impact on individuals, communities, and the environment.

Promote human values: Align AI systems with human values such as fairness, justice, privacy, and autonomy. Avoid creating systems that reinforce harmful biases or discriminate against certain groups.

Human oversight: Maintain human oversight in AI systems, especially in critical decision-making processes. Ensure that humans have the ability to intervene or override AI when necessary.

2. Fairness and Non-discrimination:

Identify and mitigate bias: Actively identify and mitigate biases in training data and algorithms to ensure fair and equitable outcomes.

Promote inclusivity: Design AI systems that are inclusive and accessible to all, regardless of background, abilities, or circumstances.

Avoid discrimination: Ensure that AI systems do not perpetuate or amplify existing social inequalities or discriminate against individuals or groups.

3. Privacy and Security:

Protect data: Implement strong data protection measures to safeguard user privacy and prevent unauthorized access to sensitive information.

Transparency and control: Provide users with transparency and control over how their data is used by AI systems.

Security measures: Implement robust security measures to protect AI systems from attacks and misuse.

4. Transparency and Explainability:

Explainable AI: Strive to make AI systems more transparent and understandable to users. Provide explanations for AI decisions and actions.

Open communication: Communicate openly about the capabilities and limitations of AI systems. Avoid misleading claims or hype.

Accountability: Establish clear lines of responsibility and accountability for AI systems and their outcomes.

5. Accountability and Responsibility:

Identify responsible parties: Clearly define the roles and responsibilities of developers, deployers, and users of AI systems.

Mechanisms for redress: Establish mechanisms for addressing unintended consequences or harms caused by AI systems.

Continuous monitoring: Continuously monitor AI systems for potential ethical issues and take corrective action when necessary.

6. Sustainability and Environmental Responsibility:

Resource efficiency: Develop AI systems that are resource-efficient and minimize their environmental impact.

Sustainable development: Use AI to promote sustainable development goals and address environmental challenges.

7. Collaboration and Governance:

Multi-stakeholder engagement: Foster collaboration among researchers, developers, policymakers, and the public to ensure ethical AI development.

Ethical guidelines and standards: Develop and adhere to ethical guidelines and standards for AI development and deployment.

International cooperation: Promote international cooperation on AI ethics to address global challenges and ensure responsible innovation.

By adhering to these guidelines, we can foster the development and deployment of ethical AI that benefits humanity and contributes to a more just and sustainable future.

Chapter 9

The Future of Qwen and Large Language Models

9.1 Emerging Trends and Research Directions

The field of AI is constantly evolving, and LLMs like Qwen 2.5 are at the forefront of this exciting revolution. Here are some of the emerging trends and research directions that are shaping the future of LLMs:

1. Enhanced Reasoning and Problem-Solving:

Neuro-symbolic AI: Combining neural networks with symbolic reasoning to enable LLMs to understand and reason about complex concepts, solve problems more effectively, and handle tasks that require logical deduction.

Commonsense Reasoning: Improving LLMs' ability to understand and apply common sense knowledge, enabling them to better navigate real-world situations and make more informed decisions.

Causal Inference: Developing LLMs that can understand cause-and-effect relationships, allowing them to make predictions and generate explanations with greater accuracy.

2. Multimodal Learning and Understanding:

Vision-Language Models: Integrating visual and textual information to enable LLMs to understand images, videos, and other visual inputs, leading to more comprehensive and nuanced understanding of the world.

Audio-Language Models: Combining audio and text processing to allow LLMs to understand spoken language, generate speech, and engage in more natural and interactive conversations.

Embodied AI: Developing LLMs that can interact with the physical world through robots or virtual agents, leading to more realistic and engaging AI experiences.

3. Personalized and Adaptive AI:

Personalized LLMs: Tailoring LLMs to individual users' preferences, learning styles, and needs, creating more personalized and effective AI assistants.

Adaptive Learning: Developing LLMs that can continuously learn and adapt to new information and changing environments, improving their performance over time.

Human-AI Collaboration: Exploring new ways for humans and AI to collaborate and complement each other's strengths, leading to more productive and creative partnerships.

4. Ethical and Responsible AI:

Fairness and Explainability: Developing techniques to ensure fairness, transparency, and accountability in LLMs, mitigating bias and promoting ethical AI development.

Robustness and Safety: Improving the robustness and safety of LLMs, making them more resilient to adversarial attacks and preventing unintended consequences.

Social Impact: Studying the societal impact of LLMs and developing strategies to ensure their responsible and beneficial use.

5. Efficient and Scalable LLMs:

Model Compression: Developing techniques to compress large LLMs, making them more efficient and accessible for deployment on various devices and platforms.

Energy-Efficient Training: Exploring new methods for training LLMs with reduced energy consumption, minimizing their environmental impact.

Hardware Acceleration: Leveraging specialized hardware to accelerate LLM training and inference, improving performance and reducing costs.

These are just a few of the exciting trends and research directions that are shaping the future of LLMs. As these technologies continue to advance, we can expect even more innovative applications and transformative impacts on various aspects of our lives.

9.2 The Potential Impact of LLMs on Society

LLMs like Qwen 2.5 are poised to have a profound and multifaceted impact on society. Here's a glimpse into some of the key areas where these powerful language models could bring about significant changes:

1. Communication and Information Access:

Breaking down language barriers: LLMs can facilitate seamless communication across different languages, fostering greater understanding and collaboration on a global scale.

Personalized information access: LLMs can curate and summarize information tailored to individual needs and preferences, making it easier for people to access relevant knowledge and insights.

Enhanced accessibility: LLMs can assist individuals with disabilities by providing text-to-speech, speech-to-text, and other assistive technologies, promoting greater inclusivity and accessibility.

2. Education and Learning:

Personalized learning: LLMs can create customized learning experiences tailored to individual students' needs and learning styles, leading to more effective and engaging education.

AI tutors and mentors: LLMs can act as virtual tutors and mentors, providing personalized guidance and support to learners of all ages.

Automated content creation: LLMs can assist educators in creating engaging educational materials, such as quizzes, summaries, and presentations, freeing up their time to focus on student interaction and individualized instruction.

3. Creativity and Innovation:

New forms of artistic expression: LLMs can generate creative content, such as poems, scripts, and musical pieces, pushing the boundaries of artistic expression and inspiring new forms of creativity.

Accelerated research and development: LLMs can assist researchers in analyzing data, generating hypotheses, and writing reports, accelerating scientific discovery and innovation.

Enhanced productivity: LLMs can automate tedious tasks, freeing up human creativity and allowing individuals to focus on higher-level thinking and problem-solving.

4. Business and the Economy:

Improved customer service: LLMs can power chatbots and virtual assistants, providing efficient and personalized customer support.

Automated content creation: LLMs can generate marketing materials, product descriptions, and other business content, increasing efficiency and productivity.

Data analysis and decision-making: LLMs can analyze large datasets and provide insights to support business decisions, leading to improved strategies and outcomes.

5. Social Good and Sustainability:

Addressing social challenges: LLMs can be used to analyze social issues, identify trends, and develop solutions to address challenges such as poverty, inequality, and climate change.

Promoting public health: LLMs can assist in disease surveillance, drug discovery, and patient education, contributing to improved public health outcomes.

Environmental conservation: LLMs can analyze environmental data, model climate change scenarios, and support conservation efforts, promoting a more sustainable future.

Challenges and Considerations:

While the potential benefits of LLMs are vast, it's important to acknowledge the potential challenges and address them proactively. These include:

Ethical considerations: Ensuring fairness, transparency, and accountability in LLM development and deployment.

Job displacement: Managing the potential impact of LLMs on the workforce and providing support for workers in transitioning to new roles.

Misinformation and misuse: Preventing the use of LLMs for malicious purposes, such as generating fake news or spreading propaganda.

By carefully considering these challenges and taking proactive steps to mitigate potential risks, we can harness the transformative power of LLMs to create a more informed, equitable, and sustainable future for all.

9.3 Qwen 2.5 in the Evolving AI Landscape

Qwen 2.5 is making a splash in the evolving AI landscape, and for good reason! Here's how it fits into the bigger picture:

1. The Rise of Open-Source LLMs:

Qwen 2.5 as a key player: Qwen 2.5, with its impressive performance and open-source nature, is challenging the dominance of closed models like GPT-4. This shift towards open access is democratizing AI, allowing more researchers, developers, and businesses to leverage powerful LLMs.

Driving innovation: Open-source models foster collaboration and accelerate innovation by enabling the community to contribute to model development, fine-tuning, and application exploration.

2. Specialization and Customization:

Tailored to specific tasks: Qwen 2.5 offers specialized variants like Qwen 2.5-Coder and Qwen 2.5-Math, catering to specific needs like code generation and mathematical reasoning. This trend towards specialization allows for more targeted and effective AI solutions.

Fine-tuning for unique applications: Qwen 2.5's open nature enables users to fine-tune the model on their own data, customizing it for specific domains and use cases. This allows businesses and researchers to create AI solutions tailored to their unique requirements.

3. Pushing the Boundaries of Performance:

Competitive performance: Qwen 2.5 demonstrates impressive performance on various benchmarks, rivaling or even surpassing some of the leading closed models. This continuous improvement in performance is pushing the boundaries of what LLMs can achieve.

Long context window: With its 1 million token context window, Qwen 2.5 can handle significantly longer pieces of text, enabling more comprehensive and nuanced understanding of information.

4. Expanding Accessibility:

Reduced barriers to entry: Open-source models like Qwen 2.5 lower the barriers to entry for individuals and organizations looking to leverage powerful AI capabilities.

Community-driven development: The open-source community contributes to model improvement, documentation, and resource creation, making LLMs more accessible and user-friendly.

5. Addressing Ethical Concerns:

Transparency and accountability: Open-source models promote transparency and allow for greater scrutiny of the model's architecture and training data, which can help identify and address potential biases.

Community-driven ethical considerations: The open-source community plays a crucial role in raising awareness of ethical concerns and promoting responsible AI development.

Qwen 2.5's Role in the Future:

Qwen 2.5 is contributing to a future where AI is more accessible, customizable, and powerful. By fostering open collaboration and pushing the boundaries of performance, Qwen 2.5 is helping to shape an AI landscape that benefits a wider range of users and applications. As the technology continues to evolve, Qwen 2.5 and other open-source LLMs will play a crucial role in democratizing AI and driving innovation across various fields.

Chapter 10

Qwen 2.5 Resources and Community

10.1 Official Documentation and Support Channels

You're looking for the Qwen 2.5 manuals! Here are the primary resources to find documentation and get support:

1. Qwen Official Website:

qwen2.org: This is the central hub for all things Qwen. You'll likely find introductory information, model overviews, and links to other important resources.

2. Qwen GitHub Repository:

github.com/QwenLM/Qwen2.5: The GitHub repo is essential for technical details. Expect to find:

Model cards with specific information about each variant (e.g., Qwen2.5-7B, Qwen2.5-Coder).

Code examples for using the models with different libraries (e.g., Transformers, vLLM).

Instructions for fine-tuning Qwen 2.5 on your own datasets.

Possibly links to community discussions or forums.

3. Hugging Face Model Hub:

huggingface.co/Qwen: Hugging Face often hosts pre-trained weights and tokenizers for popular models. You might find:

Downloadable model files.

Easy-to-use integration with the `transformers` library.

Community-contributed examples and spaces.

4. ModelScope:

modelscope.cn: This is Alibaba Cloud's platform for AI models. You might find:

Model pages with descriptions and usage instructions.

APIs for accessing Qwen 2.5 programmatically.

Potentially cloud-based deployment options.

5. Community Channels:

Discord: Many AI projects have active Discord servers. Look for an official Qwen server for community support, discussions, and announcements.

Tips for Navigating Documentation:

Start with the basics: Begin with the official website or GitHub README to get a general overview of the model and its capabilities.

Look for code examples: Code examples are often the quickest way to understand how to use the model in practice.

Check the issues: If you encounter problems, search the GitHub issues to see if others have experienced similar challenges.

Join the community: Engage with the community on Discord or other platforms to ask questions and get support from other users.

By exploring these resources and actively engaging with the Qwen 2.5 community, you'll be well-equipped to understand and effectively utilize this powerful language model.

10.2 Online Communities and Developer Forums

It's always helpful to connect with fellow developers and enthusiasts! Here are some online communities and developer forums where you can discuss Qwen 2.5, find solutions, and share your experiences:

1. Qwen Official Channels (if available):

Qwen Discord Server: Look for an official Qwen Discord server. This is often the best place for real-time discussions, quick questions, and announcements from the developers.

Qwen Forum (if they have one): Some AI projects have dedicated forums on their websites for more structured discussions and knowledge sharing.

2. General AI and LLM Communities:

Hugging Face Forums: Hugging Face has a very active community forum where you can discuss various LLMs, including Qwen 2.5. You can find sections dedicated to specific models, as well as general discussions about natural language processing and AI.

Reddit: Subreddits like r/artificialintelligence, r/LanguageTechnology, and r/MachineLearning are good places to find news, research papers, and discussions about LLMs. You might find specific threads about Qwen 2.5 or related topics.

3. Developer-Focused Platforms:

Stack Overflow: While not specifically for LLMs, Stack Overflow is a great resource for finding answers to coding questions. If you encounter any technical challenges while using Qwen 2.5, you might find solutions or get help from other developers on Stack Overflow.

GitHub Discussions: Check the Qwen 2.5 GitHub repository for a "Discussions" tab. This is a good place to ask questions, share your projects, and engage with other developers working with the model.

4. Social Media:

Twitter: Follow researchers, developers, and organizations working on LLMs (including the creators of Qwen 2.5, if they have a presence). Twitter can be a good source of news, updates, and discussions about the latest advancements in the field.

Tips for Engaging in Communities:

Be respectful and constructive: Contribute to positive and helpful discussions.

Search before asking: Check if your question has already been answered.

Share your knowledge: Help others by answering questions and sharing your experiences.

Provide context: When asking questions, give clear details about your problem or use case.

By actively participating in these online communities, you can stay updated on the latest developments in Qwen 2.5, learn from other users, and contribute to the growing knowledge base around this powerful language model.

10.3 Continuing Your Qwen 2.5 Learning Journey

It's great you're eager to continue your Qwen 2.5 learning journey! The world of LLMs is constantly evolving, so staying up-to-date and deepening your knowledge is key. Here's a roadmap to guide your ongoing exploration:

1. Master the Fundamentals:

Deepen your understanding of LLMs: Explore resources that explain the underlying architecture of LLMs, such as transformer networks, attention mechanisms, and the training process.

Refine your prompt engineering skills: Experiment with different prompting techniques (few-shot learning, chain-of-thought prompting, etc.) to elicit the best possible outputs from Qwen 2.5.

Familiarize yourself with the Qwen 2.5 ecosystem: Explore the different model variants (Qwen2.5, Qwen2.5-Coder, Qwen2.5-Math), understand their strengths and weaknesses, and choose the right model for your specific tasks.

2. Explore Advanced Topics:

Fine-tuning and customization: Learn how to fine-tune Qwen 2.5 on your own datasets to adapt it to specific domains and improve its performance on specialized tasks.

Model evaluation and analysis: Dive into techniques for evaluating LLM performance, including metrics like BLEU, ROUGE, and human evaluation.

Ethical considerations and bias mitigation: Deepen your understanding of ethical challenges related to LLMs and explore techniques for mitigating bias and ensuring fairness.

3. Stay Updated with the Latest Developments:

Follow Qwen 2.5 updates: Keep an eye on the official Qwen website, GitHub repository, and community channels for announcements about new releases, features, and research findings.

Engage with the LLM community: Participate in online forums, attend conferences, and follow researchers and developers on social media to stay informed about the latest advancements in the field.

Read research papers and publications: Explore academic publications and pre-print servers (like arXiv) to learn about cutting-edge research on LLMs and their applications.

4. Build and Experiment:

Develop your own applications: Put your knowledge into practice by building your own applications using Qwen 2.5, such as chatbots, content generators, or code assistants.

Contribute to the open-source community: Share your projects, code, and insights with the Qwen 2.5 community to contribute to the collective knowledge and advancement of the model.

Experiment with new ideas: Explore creative and innovative ways to use LLMs, pushing the boundaries of what's possible and contributing to the development of new applications.

5. Continuous Learning:

Embrace lifelong learning: The field of AI is constantly evolving, so cultivate a mindset of continuous learning and stay curious about new developments.

Share your knowledge: Teach others about LLMs and their potential, contributing to a wider understanding and adoption of these powerful technologies.

By following this roadmap and actively engaging with the Qwen 2.5 community, you can continue your learning journey and become a proficient user and contributor in the exciting world of large language models.

www.ingramcontent.com/pod-product-compliance
Lightning Source LLC
La Vergne TN
LVHW051740050326
832903LV00023B/1019